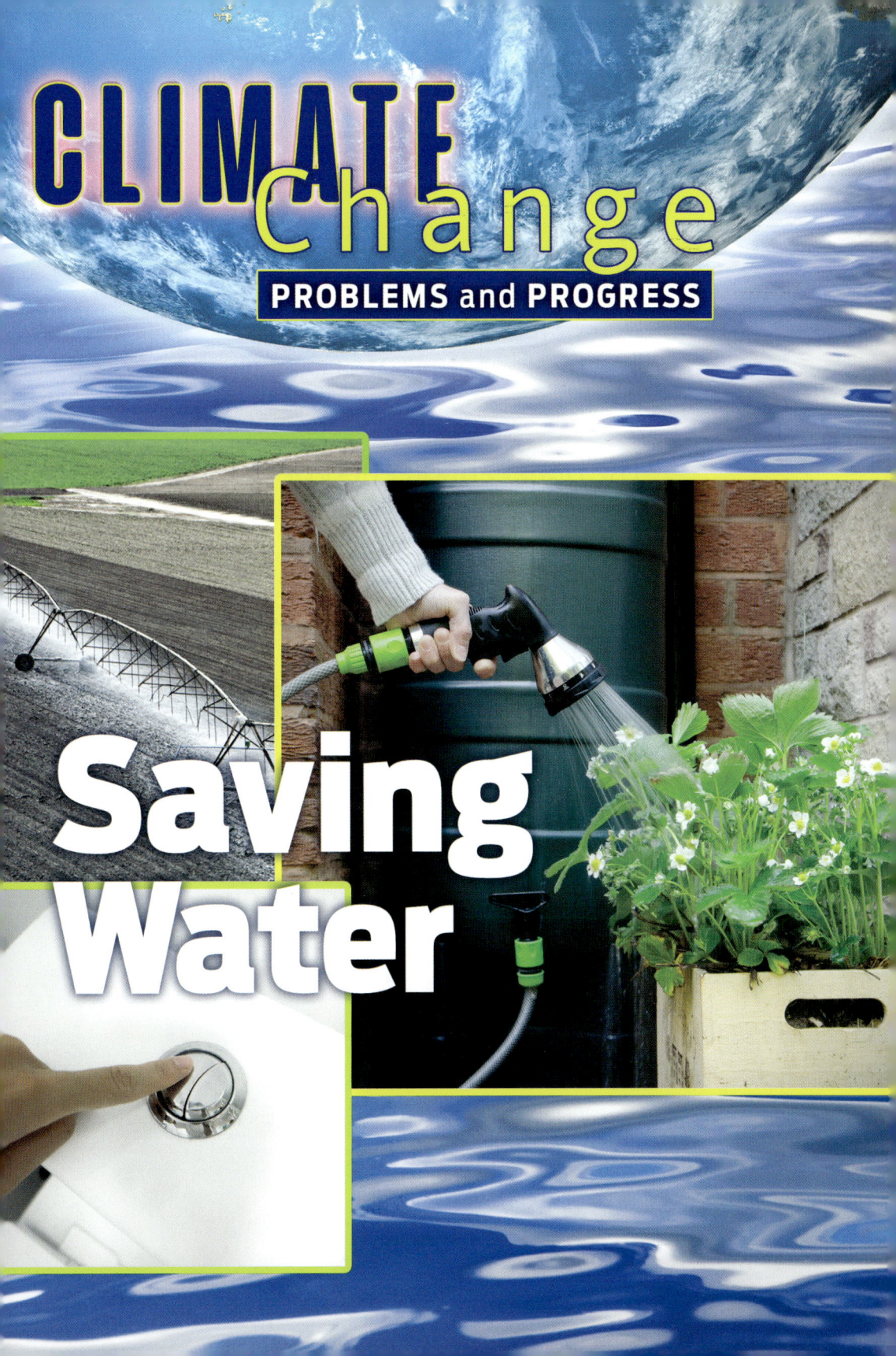

CLIMATE Change
PROBLEMS and PROGRESS

Saving Water

CLIMATE Change
PROBLEMS and PROGRESS

The Danger of Greenhouse Gases

Extreme Weather

The Future of Biodiversity

The Organic Lifestyle

Preserving Energy

Recycling Works!

Renewable Energy in Action

Saving Water

The Vital Role of Deserts and Forests

What Is Climate Change?

WITHDRAWN

CLIMATE Change
PROBLEMS and PROGRESS

Saving Water

James Shoals

Mason Crest

Mason Crest
450 Parkway Drive, Suite D
Broomall, PA 19008
www.masoncrest.com

© 2020 by Mason Crest, an imprint of National Highlights, Inc.

All rights reserved. No part of this publication may be reproduced or transmitted in any form or by any means, electronic or mechanical, including photocopying, recording, taping, or any information storage and retrieval system, without permission from the publisher.

Printed and bound in the United States of America.

Series ISBN: 978-1-4222-4353-4
Hardback ISBN: 978-1-4222-4361-9
EBook ISBN: 978-1-4222-7456-9

First printing
1 3 5 7 9 8 6 4 2

Cover photographs by Dreamstime.com: William Perry (bkgd); Martesia Bezuidenhout (top left); Shutterstock.com: DJTaylor (right); HelloRF Zcool (bottom left).

Library of Congress Cataloging-in-Publication Data is on file with the publisher.

QR Codes disclaimer:

You may gain access to certain third party content ("Third-Party Sites") by scanning and using the QR Codes that appear in this publication (the "QR Codes"). We do not operate or control in any respect any information, products, or services on such Third-Party Sites linked to by us via the QR Codes included in this publication, and we assume no responsibility for any materials you may access using the QR Codes. Your use of the QR Codes may be subject to terms, limitations, or restrictions set forth in the applicable terms of use or otherwise established by the owners of the Third-Party Sites. Our linking to such Third-Party Sites via the QR Codes does not imply an endorsement or sponsorship of such Third-Party Sites, or the information, products, or services offered on or through the Third-Party Sites, nor does it imply an endorsement or sponsorship of this publication by the owners of such Third-Party Sites.

CONTENTS

Words to Understand............ 6
Introduction................. 8
Freshwater Resources......... 10
Water Stressors 12
Global Warming & Freshwater Resources......... 14
Water for Agriculture 16
Industrial Uses................ 18
Efficient Irrigation............ 20
Gardens and Lawns........... 22
Rainwater Harvesting 24
Recycled Water............... 26
Recycling Grey Water 28
Desalinization 30
Seawater Greenhouse 32
Save Water, Save Energy 34
Saving Water at Home......... 36
Saving Water in Schools 38
Waterless Technologies........ 40
Easy Ways to Save Water....... 42

Text-Dependent Questions........ 44
Research Projects.............. 45
Find Out More 46
Series Glossary of Key Terms 47
Index........................ 48

KEY ICONS TO LOOK FOR

Words to Understand: These words with their easy-to-understand definitions will increase the reader's understanding of the text, while building vocabulary skills.

Sidebars: This boxed material within the main text allows readers to build knowledge, gain insights, explore possibilities, and broaden their perspectives by weaving together additional information to provide realistic and holistic perspectives.

Educational Videos: Readers can view videos by scanning our QR codes, providing them with additional educational content to supplement the text. Examples include news coverage, moments in history, speeches, iconic moments, and much more!

Text-Dependent Questions: These questions send the reader back to the text for more careful attention to the evidence presented here.

Research Projects: Readers are pointed toward areas of further inquiry connected to each chapter. Suggestions are provided for projects that encourage deeper research and analysis.

Series Glossary of Key Terms: This back-of-the-book glossary contains terminology used throughout this series. Words found here increase the reader's ability to read and comprehend higher-level books and articles in this field.

WORDS TO UNDERSTAND

aerator an apparatus for exposing something to the air

arid lacking sufficient water or rainfall

chlorine a common nonmetallic element used to purify water and as a bleaching agent and disinfectant

debris the remains of something that has been destroyed or broken up

distilled remove impurities from, increase the concentration of, and separate through the process of distillation

dripper a device that discharges water on the area that needs to be irrigated

efficient being effective without wasting time, effort, or expense

faucet a regulator for controlling the flow of a liquid from a reservoir

gravel rock fragments and pebbles

hydrophobic tending to repel, and not absorb water or become wet by water

impending close in time; about to occur

intrude enter uninvited

migration the movement of persons from one country or locality to another

native originated in the same geographic region

porous able to absorb fluids

recreational engaged in as a pastime

replenished fill something that had previously been emptied

seepage the process of passing gradually or leaking through

semipermeable selectively allowing fluids to pass through

sensor any device that receives a signal or stimulus (as heat, or pressure, or light, or motion, etc.) and responds to it in a specific manner

sieve a filter to retain larger pieces while liquids pass through

solvent a liquid substance capable of dissolving other substances

stressors processes or events that cause stress

thermoelectric electricity produced by heat

valve a mechanical device for controlling the flow of a fluid

percolate pass through

urbanization the social process whereby cities grow and societies become more urban

wetland a low area where the land is saturated with water

INTRODUCTION

Water is an essential component for humans as well as animals. Thus, it is important to save water for the future. Rapid climate change is drastically altering weather patterns around the world and affecting the quantity as well as the quality of water resources. Pollution, population explosion, and **urbanization** are other major factors putting stress on the available freshwater resources.

The treatment of dirty water consumes huge amounts of energy in the form of electricity and fuel. By conserving and using freshwater efficiently, humans could save a lot of energy that is utilized for water treatment and transportation. They could also avoid a potential water crisis in the future when the demand for water would exceed its supply considerably.

Importance of Water

Only a **marginal** quantity of the total water available on earth is drinkable or usable for agricultural, industrial, and domestic purposes. The consumption of freshwater has increased ten times since 1900, whereas its supply is gradually decreasing due to global warming. If water is not conserved in the present, we may face a severe water crisis in the future.

Crisis, Stress, and Scarcity

When the water demand of an area exceeds the availability, it indicates a water crisis. Many regions are presently suffering from water crises, even though the earth has enough freshwater to meet global requirements. It is due to the uneven **distribution** of water in the world, wastage, increasing water pollution, and global warming. When the annual water supply for a person in an area goes below 60,000 cubic feet (1,700 cubic m), it is called water stress; when it drops down to 35,000 cubic feet(1,000 cubic m per person, it is called water scarcity.

Current Condition

At present, more than 1.3 billion people in the world are living in areas where there is a physical shortage of water. About 1.6 billion people are facing economic water shortage, which means that their countries lack the monetary means to efficiently draw water from rivers and underground. Most of sub-Saharan Africa faces a similar situation. It is estimated that by 2025, 1.8 billion people will live in areas with water scarcity.

Climate Facts

- On average, an Australian **consumes** almost 264 thousand gallons (1 milllion l) of freshwater annually.
- By 2025, about two-thirds of the global population will be living in water-stressed regions if water is not conserved.

Saving Water

Freshwater Resources

The earth is popularly known as the "blue planet" since 75 percent of it is covered with water. Out of this, about 97 percent is salty and the remaining is usable freshwater. About 68.7 percent of freshwater is locked in ice sheets and glaciers found in Antarctica, Greenland, the Arctic, and the Himalayas. The remaining is unevenly distributed across the world.

Surface Water

Lakes, rivers, and freshwater **wetlands** together form the surface water that accounts for 0.9 percent of the total freshwater. Humans draw water from these sources for drinking, agricultural, and other purposes. These are renewable sources that replenish themselves through rainfall and snowfall. However, **overextraction** of water, pollution, and changes in climate patterns due to global warming are severely disturbing their replenishment and decreasing their quantity.

10 CLIMATE CHANGE: Problems and Progress

How aquifers work

Groundwater

About 30.1 percent of the total freshwater is found deep below the earth's surface in layers of rocks and soil. These layers with water are called aquifers. Water is **replenished** in these layers through seepage from the surface water. Groundwater is mostly used for drinking purposes and is drawn through hand pumps, motor pumps, and wells. It is the cleanest source of potable water, but global warming is affecting its quality as well.

Climate Facts

- Brazil has the largest supply of freshwater, followed by Russia and Canada.

- More than a billion people depend on the rivers flowing from the Himalayas for freshwater.

Saving Water

Water Stressors

Many countries suffer from water shortage because they do not have sufficient water sources. However, there are many countries with adequate freshwater that still face water scarcity. This is due to water **stressors** that put pressure on the available water. To avoid such a situation, water needs to be used carefully and water stressors need to be managed.

Major Water Stressors

Overpopulation, especially in developing countries, is putting more pressure on water resources. Global population is predicted to increase by about three billion by 2050, out of which 90 percent is expected to live in developing countries. The **migration** of people to regions with sufficient water supply is another stressor that increases water demand and eventually pushes that region toward water stress. At present, there are more than 191 million migrants worldwide. Changes in precipitation patterns due to global warming are also contributing to water stress.

12 CLIMATE CHANGE: Problems and Progress

Economic Development

With rapid global economic development, water **consumption** is increasing quickly. The use of virtual water (found in a finished product or used during the production of a product) is increasing tremendously with the development of industries such as business, tourism, entertainment, and others. Currently, virtual water accounts for 40 percent of the global water consumption.

Climate Facts

- Annually, the global population increases by about eighty million. In the past 50 years, water usage has tripled.

- In several European cities with populations of over 100,000, **groundwater** is used at a much faster rate than it is recharged.

Saving Water 13

Global Warming & Freshwater Resources

Rising global temperatures are increasing **freshwater** requirements and thus putting stress on its availability. The quantity as well as the quality of water is degrading at an alarming rate, making way for a future water crisis. To avoid the shortage of freshwater, efforts to control global warming should be stepped up.

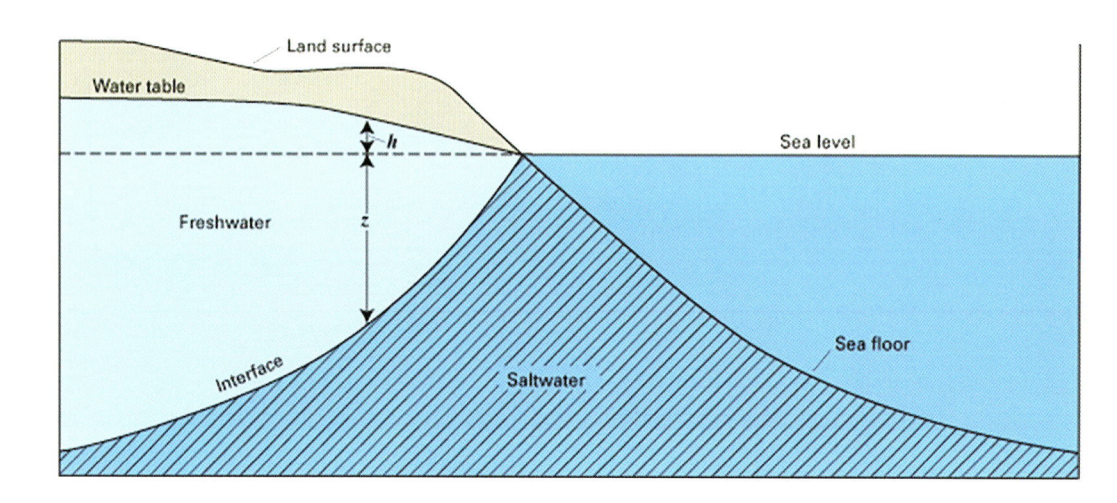

Increasing Salinity

Sea levels are rising due to the expansion of water caused by excess warming and the melting of glaciers. This is causing saline water to **intrude** into the surface waters and the aquifers on the Gulf, Pacific, and Atlantic coasts. This is degrading the freshwater quality and in turn affecting the coastal population's health.

14   CLIMATE CHANGE: Problems and Progress

Effect on Groundwater

With increasing evaporation and the frequent occurrence of droughts, water levels of aquifers are drastically dropping in many countries. In regions where rainfall and floods occur more often, the aquifers are not getting recharged as most of the water is drained away and does not **percolate** through the soil.

Water Levels of Lakes

Due to rising temperatures, the amount of precipitation is decreasing in certain regions and the evaporation of water from plants and soils is increasing. It is causing the water levels of various lakes to descend. Scientists have predicted that the water levels of Lake Huron and Lake Michigan in central North America will decrease by about 4.5 ft. (1.37 m) in the next century.

Climate Facts

- Since the 1890s, there has been an average rise of 6 to 9 in. (17.5 cm) in sea levels.

- The aquifer levels in cities like Bangkok, Beijing, Shanghai, Madras, and Mexico have dropped between 16-35 yds. (15-50 m).

Saving Water

Water for Agriculture

Agriculture alone accounts for about 70 percent of global freshwater withdrawals from lakes, aquifers, and rivers. The reduction in freshwater resources drastically affects global food production. In order to keep food production and food prices stable, water needs to be conserved and managed wisely.

Rainfed Agriculture

In this type of agriculture, farmers depend on rainwater, also called green water, for irrigating crops. Most countries around the world heavily depend on rainwater for producing major crops like wheat, rice, and maize. About 80 percent of the global cultivated area is rainfed, and it accounts for 60 percent of the total crop production. Rainfed agriculture does not affect other sectors that require freshwater.

Irrigated Agriculture

In this type of agriculture, the water used for crop production is drawn from surface and ground waters, also called blue water. Even though only 20 percent of global cultivated land is irrigated by blue water, it competes heavily with the other sectors for freshwater. Increased groundwater withdrawal for agriculture is depleting aquifers at a faster rate than they are **replenished**. The Great Plains in the United States, the North China Plain, and Punjab in India are likely to suffer losses in crop production in the future if water withdrawals are not controlled in the present.

Water Loss in Irrigation

Despite difficulties in the management of irrigation systems, as well as their failure in some parts of the world, there is a growing demand to increase irrigation. However, the key lies in an **efficient** use of water. At present, 60 percent of the water used in irrigation is lost before it reaches crops due to **seepage** and evaporation. The growing pressure on freshwater can be reduced if irrigation systems are managed more efficiently and waterlogging and salinization are prevented.

Climate Facts

- Rainfed agriculture covers about 90 percent of the cultivated land in Latin America, 95 percent in sub-Saharan Africa, and 65 percent in East Asia.

- At present, more than 1.25 million sq. miles (3,245,566 sq km) of global land is irrigated by ground and surface water.

Saving Water

Industrial Uses

Besides agriculture, there are other sectors that heavily depend on freshwater, such as industries, recreation, and others. Since global warming is affecting the quantity and quality of freshwater, these sectors are hard-pressed to find ways to recycle water and conserve it to save the future of their businesses.

Industrial Sector

About 22 percent of the freshwater worldwide is used by various industries. It is used in **thermoelectric** power plants, chemical processes in oil refineries, and as a **solvent** in manufacturing companies. All these industries discharge their wastewater into nearby rivers and cause pollution. Lawmakers around the world have put strict regulations on industries to treat their wastewater and return it to the environment.

Recreational Sector

Water is used for **recreational** activities like sailing, water skiing, swimming, diving, surfing, and golf. In golf, a large quantity of water is used for maintaining green grounds. In all these activities except golf, water is not consumed. However, the use of freshwater in these activities limits its availability to more important sectors such as agriculture and industries.

Thermal Power Plants

One of the largest uses of water worldwide is in thermal power plants. Here, steam-driven turbine generators are used for generating electricity. The cooling of power-producing equipment also requires large quantities of water. Since the water used in this process gets heated up tremendously, it cannot be released back into the environment.

Climate Facts

- In a single day, the United States uses around 346 billion gallons (1.3 trillion l) of freshwater.
- To refine one barrel of oil, about 1,850 gallons (7,000 l) of freshwater is used.

Saving Water 19

Efficient Irrigation

In the last forty years, many countries have started using improved plant varieties that produce more crops per drop of water, and are practicing water-efficient irrigation methods. This has almost doubled the crop yields in those countries. In 2005, Europe's cereal production was five tons per hectare due to improved crop practices.

Deficit Irrigation

Farmers in different countries are aware of the **impending** water crisis that will force them to grow crops under water stress. To cope with such a situation, deficit irrigation methods have been developed. These methods focus on increasing the crop growth per unit of water. Under these methods, less water is supplied to the crops than they require. This puts a little stress on crops and makes them drought-tolerant. This way, huge amount of water is saved with much less impact on the total crop production. Crops less sensitive to water stress such as cotton, maize, groundnuts, wheat, and sugar beets can adapt to deficit irrigation practices.

Irrigation in Africa

CLIMATE CHANGE: Problems and Progress

Drip Irrigation

Drip irrigation method (DIM), also known as trickle irrigation, is a modern irrigation technique used by farmers in water scarce areas. It involves dripping water very slowly, drop by drop, to the roots of the crops. It is released either on the soil's surface or directly under the soil at the root region. Farmers spread the pipes across the fields and water is discharged using **valves** and **drippers**. DIM is mostly used to grow crops such as bananas, coconuts, tomatoes, grapes, strawberries, maize, cotton, and sugarcane. In India, DIM is used extensively in the horticulture belt of West Maharashtra and the cotton belt of Khandesh and Marathwada.

Climate Facts

- About 84 percent of the water withdrawal in Asia is used for agricultural purposes.
- About 260-800 gallons (1,000–3,000 l) of water are required to produce a half-pound (1 kg) of rice.

Saving Water

Gardens and Lawns

A large percentage of freshwater in households is used for irrigating landscapes, gardens, and lawns. People think that beautiful gardens can be maintained only with extensive watering and fertilization. This is not true. Some water-efficient ways to cultivate lawns can go a long way in saving water.

Minimize Turfgrass

Surface areas that are covered with a layer of grass are called turfgrass regions. These usually require huge amounts of water for maintenance. One should opt for grass that requires less amount of water, such as Turffalo grass, and should limit turfgrass to only those parts of the house that also serve as the playground for children.

Water Carefully

Manual watering is the most efficient way to irrigate lawns. It reduces water consumption by almost 34 percent less than automatic irrigation systems, such as in-ground sprinklers that release water automatically at a fixed time, and drip irrigation systems that discharge water directly at the roots of plants at preset intervals. While using automatic irrigation systems, one should install rain and soil moisture **sensors**, which prevent them from working when it is raining or the soil is moist above the preset level.

Choose Plants Wisely

One should select **native** plants for their gardens as they adjust well with the climate, soil, rainfall, and sunlight available in the region. They require minimum water and fertilizers for growth and are resistant to insects and pests as well. Opting for such plant breeds will help one to contribute their own bit in saving precious water.

Climate Facts

- In the United States, about 7.9 billion gallons (30 billion l) of water is used every day for outdoor purposes.

- Most lawns require 1 inch (25 mm) of water per week for maintenance.

Saving Water

Rainwater Harvesting

One of the best and cheapest ways to save water is rainwater harvesting. It prevents freshwater from mixing with dirty water. Moreover, it reduces stress on groundwater for meeting the various water requirements. Utilizing rainwater in sectors other than agriculture can take some stress off surface and groundwater resources.

Storage for Future

When there is a shortage of water during peak summers, rainwater can be effectively used for washing cars, cleaning houses, filling up swimming pools, and other such purposes. To do so, one needs to install rain barrels in one's home. These are PVC containers that collect rainwater from house rooftops. These have a **sieve** that prevents the entrance of **debris**, mosquitoes, and other insects into the water. Rain barrels can save more than 1,300 gallons (4,900 l) of freshwater in a typical household. The techniques of rainwater harvesting can also be effectively utilized by the recreation sector.

Immediate Use of Rainwater

Rain gardens in homes, in which rainwater collected on rooftops and driveways is channeled to gardens for irrigation, are one of the best rainwater harvesting methods. These gardens prevent rainwater from draining away to streets and filter 30 percent more water into the ground than do normal lawns. Another way of harvesting rainwater is the construction of **gravel** or **porous** pavements in houses and roads. These enable rainwater to seep into the soil, and recharge aquifers.

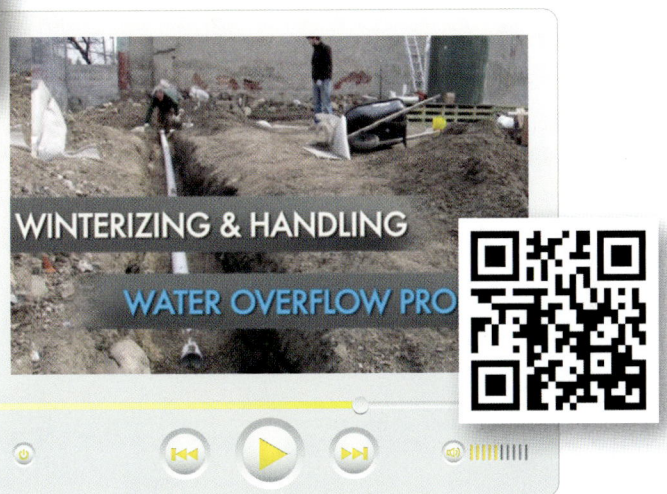

Rooftop watering system

Climate Facts

- At present, Brazil and China have the biggest rainwater harvesting systems.
- From one inch of rainfall on a roof as large as 2,000 sq. ft. (18 sq m), 1,250 gallons (4,731 l) of rainwater can be collected and reused.

Saving Water

Recycled Water

Recycled water is the treated wastewater or sewage discharged from households and industries. Its contaminants are removed in a water treatment plant. This water is sold at lower rates to encourage people to use it. Recycled water is popular in developed nations. In developing nations, however, 80 percent of sewage is discharged untreated into rivers.

Nonpotable Uses

About 36 percent of the global reclaimed water is used for irrigation in agriculture. This water contains various nutrients—oxygen, nitrogen, and phosphorus—that help in the growth of high-value crops such as wheat and maize. It is also used to irrigate lawns and golf courses. Municipal corporations in the United States and the United Kingdom utilize it for extinguishing fires and cleaning streets.

Recharging Groundwater

Even though recycled water is unhealthy for direct drinking, it can be used indirectly to increase the quantity of potable water. This is done by pumping this water into aquifers, then drawing it back and treating it. The treated water thus becomes drinkable. This process is known as groundwater recharging. Lateral shafts with bore wells are also built for this purpose.

Climate Facts

- In Singapore, reclaimed water produced by the country's Public Utilities Board is called NEWater.

- The Tel Aviv Metropolitan in Israel treats 100 percent of its sewage and reuses it for public works and in agriculture.

Saving Water

Recycling Grey Water

The wastewater generated from domestic activities such as dishwashing, bathing, and laundering is called grey water. Wastewater from toilets that contains feces and urine is called black water. Grey water can be treated and recycled for flushing toilets and irrigating lawns. However, black water cannot be recycled.

Benefits

By using recycled grey water, the use of freshwater for other purposes other than drinking and cooking can be cut down. It reduces excessive discharge of wastewater into the treatment plant, which helps in treating discharged wastewater more effectively and efficiently. Groundwater is recharged when excess grey water, used to water plants, seeps into the soils.

Proper Usage

Grey water contains dissolved soaps and detergents. Using it without treatment for irrigating gardens can have harmful effects on the growth of plants. One must only use treated grey water for flushing toilets as well, as untreated grey water leaves stains on the toilet and produces a foul smell after a few hours.

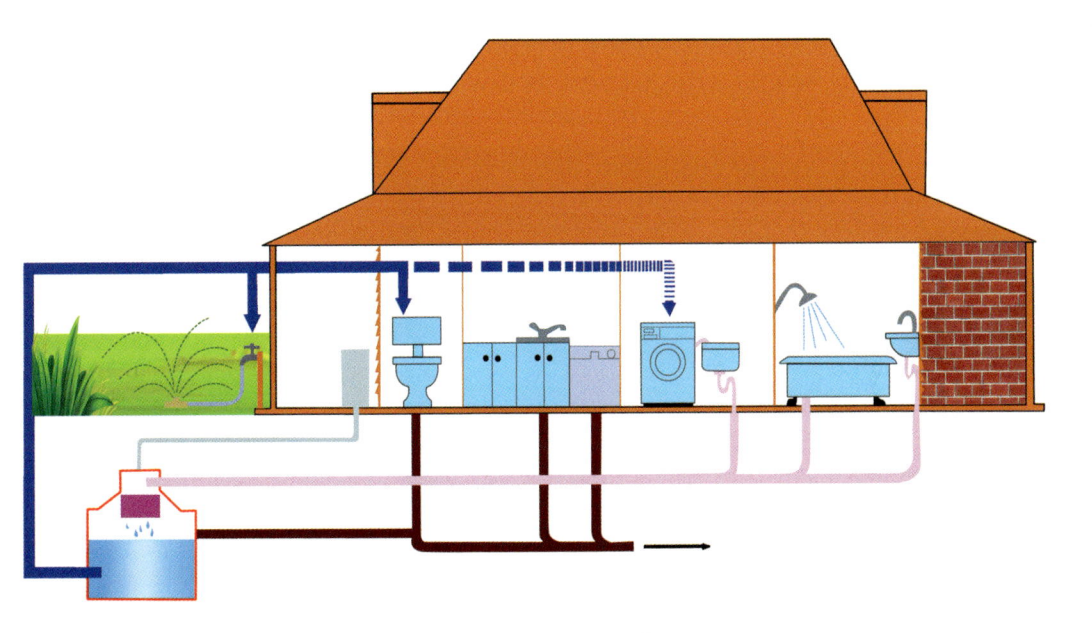

Treating Grey Water

During grey water treatment, solid pollutants are removed by passing the water through a filter. Then **chlorine** bleach is added to disinfect it. Finally, it is left undisturbed for a while, so that any solid contaminants present in it can settle and any other fats and oils may emerge on the surface, leaving treated grey water in the middle.

Climate Facts

- The use of recycled grey water reduces the annual freshwater consumption in the world by almost 45 percent.

- After 24 hours, stored grey water becomes as harmful as black water.

Saving Water   29

Desalinization

Desalinization is the process that removes salt from water and turns it into freshwater. This helps in saving groundwater for drinking purposes since other freshwater needs can be easily met by desalinated water. Desalinization plants have been constructed in countries such as Israel and Saudi Arabia, where there is always a shortage of freshwater.

Distillation

In this process, salty water is heated in large, corrosion-resistant, closed tanks. The steam generated is condensed and freshwater is obtained. To reduce the energy consumed to heat water, heat from the steam of the first tank is used to heat the water in the second tank, and so on. The Minjur Desalinization Plant in Chennai, India, is South Asia's biggest desalinization plant. It produces 43 million square yards (36.5 million cubic m) of freshwater annually.

High pressure

Semipermeable membrane

Reverse Osmosis

This is the most widely used desalinization process. In this method, a tank is divided by a **semipermeable** membrane. On the one side, salty water is placed, and on the other side, clean water is obtained. Pressure is exerted on salty water that forces the freshwater to gush out from the other side, leaving the salt behind. It is a widely used method since it purifies water up to 98 percent. About 17 percent of the potable water in Perth, Australia, is obtained from seawater by this process.

Multiple-effect Distillation

In this process, the pure water produced by heating salty water flows into the next chamber. It is boiled again by the heat energy that it carries, producing more vapor. However, this technique can only be used for small-scale desalinization.

Climate Facts

- The Jebel Ali Desalinization Plant located in the United Arab Emirates is the world's largest desalinization plant.
- Worldwide, there are 14,451 desalinization plants that produce about 72 million cubic yards (60 million cubic m) of freshwater every day.

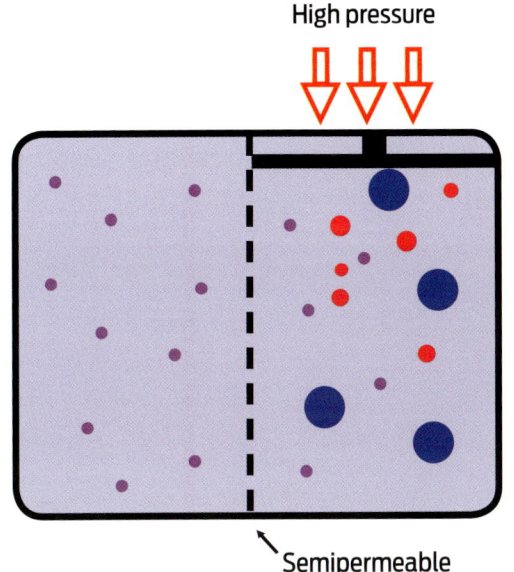

Saving Water 31

Seawater Greenhouse

To deal with the unavailability of freshwater for agriculture in certain dry regions, Charlie Paton, a British inventor, developed the seawater greenhouse technology in 1991. This technology produces freshwater from seawater and uses it for growing crops. It is economical and sustainable since it uses solar energy and seawater.

Benefits

This technology is clean and efficient since it does not require fossil fuels. The electricity used in a seawater greenhouse is generated completely by solar energy. The running cost of this greenhouse is 10 to 20 percent less than a conventional greenhouse since it produces and uses its own solar power and freshwater. It does not use fertilizers either. The nutrients present in seawater are extracted and used to fertilize the crops. The salt gained in this process can be sold, while the other minerals can be used as nutrients for crops.

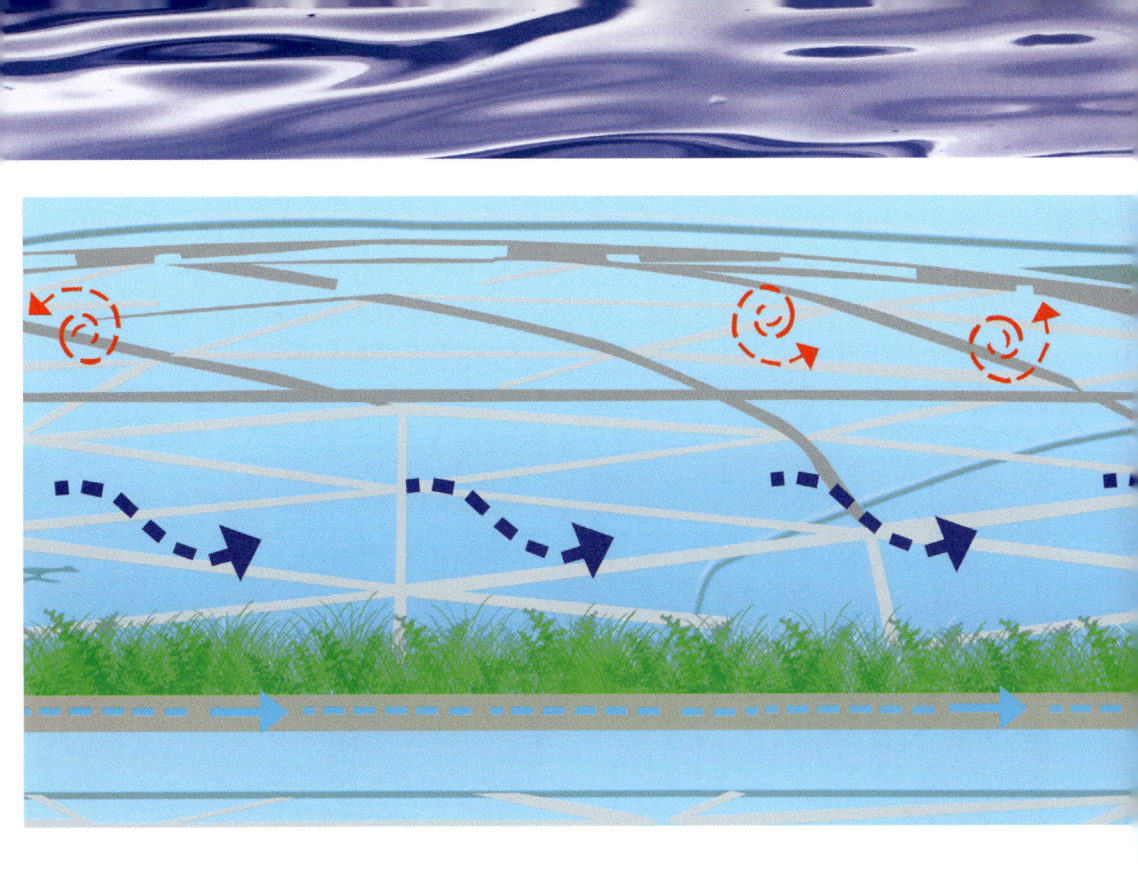

How it Works

First, seawater is pumped through the first wall of the evaporator. As air passes through this wall, it becomes cool and humid after dust and pollen are filtered. Then sunlight is selectively filtered through the roof to remove the radiation that does not help in photosynthesis. This keeps the greenhouse cool, while the crops receive the required sunlight for growth. Now the air passes through a second evaporator where it is humidified to the saturation point. The saturated air passes through a condenser, where it is cooled using cold seawater pipes. This **distilled** water condenses and is sent to storage. It is then used for irrigation.

Climate Facts

- In 2010, a seawater greenhouse called Sundrop Farms Pvt. Ltd. started operations in Australia.

- The first seawater greenhouse was built in 1992 on the Canary Islands, just off the northwestern coast of Africa.

Save Water, Save Energy

Water and energy are equally important for human survival. At present, hydroelectricity is the most commonly used form of electricity. It uses more water than any other form of energy. To safeguard the future of humans, it is important to use water wisely since energy production is heavily dependent on it.

Water for Energy

Freshwater resources play a vital role in energy production in various ways. First, surface waters are used to generate hydroelectricity. Next, large amounts of water are withdrawn to cool power plants that utilize heat to generate electricity. To generate one kilowatt of energy, about 37 to 54 gallons (140 to 204 l) of freshwater are used, depending on whether it is a nuclear or fossil fuel plant. Freshwater withdrawn to cool power plants worldwide is almost equal to the total water withdrawn for irrigating crop fields.

More Demands on Water

Enhanced oil recovery practices that are becoming very common, are quite water-intensive. Other than the extraction of oil, its processing and transportation also require water. Some new techniques designed to extract natural gas, such as hydraulic fracturing, also require water. As in the case of oil, water is used in the processing and transportation of natural gas as well. This shows that the energy demand on water resources are quite high.

Energy Efficient Equipment

Water and energy both can be saved at home by using high-efficiency washing (HEW) machines. These washing machines use 40 percent less water and 55 percent less energy than the average washer. Another simple way to save energy and water at home is by running full loads in the dishwasher as it uses about 37 percent less water than what is spent in washing dishes by hand.

Climate Facts

- In the United States, about 8 percent of total electricity is used for pumping, treating, and heating water that can power more than five million homes in a year.

- A tap left running for five minutes uses as much amount of energy as a 60-watt bulb consumes in fourteen hours.

Saving Water at Home

It may not be possible to completely avoid using freshwater for domestic purposes. However, the unchecked use of freshwater for certain household activities leads to much waste. One can easily save up to 300 gallons (1,135 l) of water a day by fixing leaky taps, toilets, and pipes.

Domestic Sector

About 8 percent of global freshwater is used for household and drinking purposes. In an urban household, about 90 gallons (340 l) of freshwater are used daily for drinking, cooking, dishwashing, laundry, sanitation, and bathing. Five to 10 gallons (18-37 l) of freshwater are used for gardening. To decrease the domestic wastage of water, people are encouraged to recycle water and use it for sanitation and watering lawns.

Kitchen and Laundry

Everyone can contribute to saving water by doing some simple things around their homes. For example, the tap should not be left running while washing vegetables or dishes by hand. An automatic dishwasher and washing machine should be used only with a full load. In case of partial loads, the water level should be adjusted accordingly instead of following the regular wash cycle that uses the same amount of water as a full load. Can grey water be saved and used in the garden? Or re-use water used to cook food such as eggs or to warm up frozen foods. Steaming food instead of boiling it uses less water, so perhaps find recipes that call for more steaming.

Faucets and Showers

About 15 percent of the water used in a house is drawn from **faucets**. Faucet **aerators** that spread water into tiny droplets should be used to avoid wastage while washing hands. General showerheads that use 2.5 gallons (9.4 l) of water per minute should be replaced with water-efficient showerheads that use about 2 gallons (7.5 l) per minute. However, it is best to use buckets for bathing since that helps to keep a check on water wastage.

Toilets

About 30 percent of water used in a household goes into flushing toilets. To save water, use water-efficient low flush or dual flush toilets. A low-flush toilet uses 1.6 gallons (6 l) of water in a single flush compared to a conventional toilet that uses 3.5 gallons (13 l). In a dual-flush toilet, there are two separate tanks, one with more water for solids and the other with less water for flushing liquids.

Climate Facts

- A dual flush toilet saves up to 67 percent of water in a household.

- Showers account for about 17 percent of water usage in a household.

Saving Water in Schools

Water is used for many purposes in schools, such as drinking, cleaning floors, and others. With so many uses, it is necessary to follow water-efficient ways to save this important resource. Young children tend to waste water due to unchecked usage; educating them how to save it is a must.

Saving Water Indoors

Schools can save large amounts of water indoors by doing the following:

- Replacing normal taps with those that turn off automatically.
- Replacing single flush toilets with dual flush toilets that use less water in each flush.
- Fixing leaks as quickly as possible.
- Installing aerators on taps to reduce the flow of water.
- Using a mop instead of a hose to clean toilet blocks.
- Doing a quarterly inspection of all taps for any leaks.

Saving Water Outdoors

Schools can save large amounts of water outdoors by:
- Planting plants and trees that require the least amount of water for maintenance.
- Applying a layer of mulch at a depth of 2.5-4 inches (7-10 cm) around plants to retain moisture in the soil and reduce evaporation by up to 70 percent.
- Using a broom instead of a hose to clean school driveways, paths, and paved areas.
- Installing a rainwater tank and using this water for cleaning purposes.

Climate Facts

- A dripping tap wastes about one drop per second, which is equal to wasting 1,850 gallons (7,000 l) of water per year.

- On average, primary and secondary schools use 8-13 square yards (7-11 sq m) of water per pupil per year.

Saving Water

Waterless Technologies

With increased awareness of the growing stress on freshwater resources and the need for water conservation, various waterless technologies have been developed so that water is used economically. These technologies are most popular in **arid** regions as well as those where water is scarce.

Waterless Urinals

Public waterless urinals do not require any water for flushing. These urinals have a **hydrophobic** chemical coating on their surface that makes the urine slip into the sewer instantly. The coating also prevents the formation of bacteria and stains on the surface. There is a non-returning valve in the drain that stops vapors from urine from coming up, preventing the occurrence of foul odors.

Waterless Car Washes

About 14 gallons (52 l) of water are required for a normal car wash, whereas waterless car wash technology washes cars without any water. It includes a series of chemical products that do the cleaning. A special wax is used to clean the body of the car, which is then wiped off using a microfiber towel that removes the toughest stains from any surface.

Waterless Washing Machines

Washing machines account for about 13 percent of the daily water used in a typical household. Waterless washing machines do not use water. They use reusable nylon polymer beads instead that look like plastic beads, to clean stains off the clothes. These beads have more stain-absorbing capacity than water. After washing, these beads are separated into a drum by the machine, leaving behind clean and dry clothes.

Climate Facts

- In Brisbane, Australia, the use of waterless urinals has been mandated due to water stress.

- Waterless washing machines use one-tenth of the water and only about 2 percent of the power used by conventional machines.

Saving Water

Easy Ways to Save Water

The work to save water starts with each and every person. If everyone did only a few of the ideas on this list every day, water scarcity and water shortage could ease over time. A lot of the solution will come from the growing awareness of the problem. Share this list with friends and family and be part of the solution.

1. Repair dripping faucets quickly.
2. Do not keep the faucet running while washing hands, face, or shaving.
3. Turn off faucets tightly when not in use.
4. Install faucet aerators that reduce water wastage by mixing water and air.
5. Avoid flushing the toilet unnecessarily.
6. Replace your showerhead with an ultra-low-flow model.
7. Avoid taking long showers.
8. Use a water-efficient dishwasher that needs only 4.5 to 7 gallons (17–26 l) per load.
9. Run the dishwasher only when it is full.
10. To clean vegetables, use the sink or a bowl to retain water.
11. Thaw frozen foods in advance in the refrigerator, or use the microwave instead of running water.
12. Use water-efficient washing machines.
13. Run the washing machine only with a full load of laundry.
14. Use a broom instead of a hose to clean your driveway or sidewalk.
15. Cover pools to reduce evaporation.
16. Water lawns at night or early morning as plants absorb more water at those times.

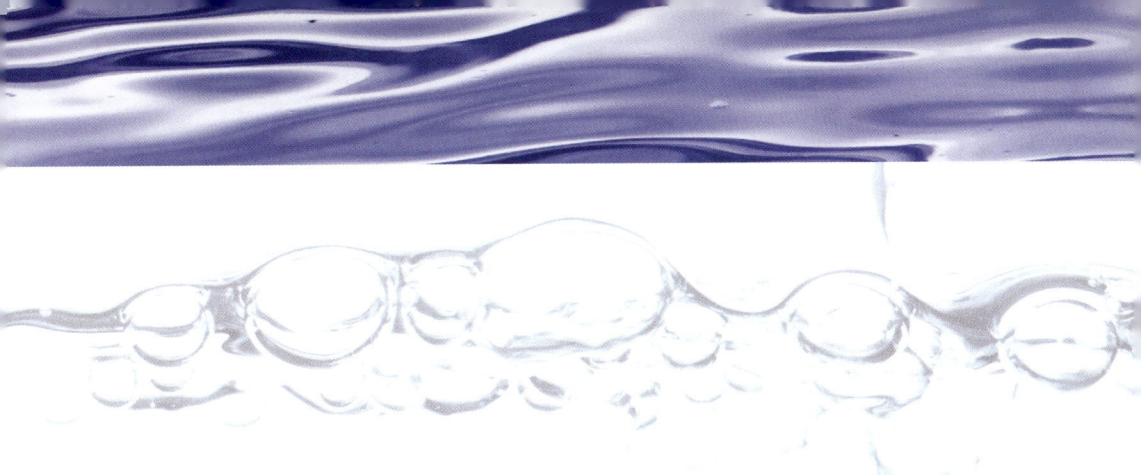

17. Check sprinkler systems and timing devices regularly to ensure that they operate properly.
18. Collect rainwater for irrigating plants, washing cars, or general cleaning projects.
19. Group plants together based on similar water needs. This will reduce over-watering of the plants that do not need as much.
20. Add compost to soil to improve its water-holding capacity.
21. Use mulch to retain moisture in the soil.
22. Choose drought-tolerant plants.
23. Collect condensed water from air-conditioning units for watering plants.
24. Adjust your lawnmower to cut grass to a height of 2.5 inches (6.35 cm). Doing so will help trap moisture and reduce the amount of watering needed.
25. When using a drinking fountain, let go of the button/handle when pausing for breath.
26. Use sprinklers to water large areas of grass. Water small patches by hand.
27. Install rainwater-harvesting devices so that the collected water can be reused.
28. Bathe your pets outdoors, in an area that needs to be watered.
29. Children should carry a water bottle to school and avoid using a drinking fountain since it can lead to wasting water.
30. Promote the conservation of water by raising awareness among users.

TEXT-DEPENDENT QUESTIONS

1. How many people are living in areas where there is a physical water shortage?

2. Give two reasons for the rise of sea levels.

3. What is an aquifer?

4. What is the word for the process of using water to grow crops?

5. Why do native plants use less water?

6. What is grey water?

7. What is desalinization?

8. How is water used to produce electricity?

RESEARCH PROJECTS

1. Where does your water come from? Research your town's or city's water supply and trace water from its source to your tap. Prepare a chart or a drawing showing the steps the water goes through.

2. Can you reduce your water usage? Keep a log of your daily use of water in all its forms. Then come up with a list of four ways you could reduce that usage. Use the tips on page 42 as a starting point.

3. As the text shows, irrigation is a major use of water. Research drought-tolerant plants and alternative ground covers and design a small garden or yard that uses little or no water for irrigation. Use plants, stones, gravel, and other natural materials (no artificial turf!).

FIND OUT MORE

Books

Kallen, Stuart. *Running Dry: The Global Water Crisis.* Mankato, MN: Twenty-First Century Books, 2015.

Moffett, Helen. *101 Water-Wise Ways.* Blackheath, South Africa: Bookstorm, 2018.

Pearce, Fred. *When the Rivers Run Dry: Water—The Defining Crisis of the Twenty-First Century (Updated Edition).* Boston: Beacon Press, 2018.

On the Internet

World Water Council
www.worldwatercouncil.org/en/water-crisis

The Water Project
thewaterproject.org/water-scarcity/

World Wildlife Fund
www.worldwildlife.org/threats/water-scarcity
An article on how water shortages affect wildlife and habitat.

SERIES GLOSSARY OF KEY TERMS

bioaccumulation the process of the buildup of toxic chemical substances in the body

biodiversity the diversity of plant and animal life in a habitat (or in the world as a whole)

ecosystem refers to a community of organisms, their interaction with each other, and their physical environment

famine a severe shortage of food (as through crop failure), resulting in hunger, starvation, and death

hydrophobic tending to repel and not absorb water

irrigation the method of providing water to agricultural fields

La Niña periodic, significant cooling of the surface waters of the equatorial Pacific Ocean, which causes abnormal weather patterns

migration the movement of persons or animals from one country or locality to another

pollutants the foreign materials which are harmful to the environment

precipitation the falling to earth of any form of water (rain, snow, hail, sleet, or mist)

stressors processes or events that cause stress

susceptible yielding readily to or capable of

symbiotic the interaction between organisms (especially of different species) that live together and happen to benefit from each other

vulnerable someone or something that can be easily harmed or attacked

INDEX

agriculture, 15, 24, 26, 32-33
aquifers, 11, 15, 18, 25, 27
car washes, 24, 40
crops, 20-21, 26, 32
deficit irrigation, 20
desalinization, 30-31
distillation, 30-31, 33
domestic sector, 36-37
drip irrigation, 21-22
economic development, 13
energy efficient equipment, 35-37
freshwater, 13, 18, 22, 24, 30, 32, 36
freshwater resources, 10-11, 34
gardens, 22-23, 25, 36
global warming, 10, 12-13, 18
grey water, 28-29, 36
groundwater, 11, 15, 18, 27-28
hydraulic fracturing, 35
hydroelectricity, 34
industrial uses, 18
irrigated agriculture, 16, 26, 34
native plants, 23
oil, 35
osmosis, 31

overpopulation, 12
Paton, Charlie, 32
power plants, 34
rainfed agriculture, 16
rainwater harvesting, 24-25
recreation, 19, 24
recycled water, 26, 28, 36
saline water, 13
saving water, 36-43
seawater greenhouse technology, 32-33
showerheads, 37
solar energy, 32
surface water, 10
thermal power plants, 18-19
toilets, 37
turfgrasses, 12, 22
urinals, 40
washing machines, 35
wastewater, 26, 28
water crisis, 8-9
water stressors, 12
water-efficiency, 22-25
waterless technologies, 40-41
wetlands, 10

Photo Credits

Photographs sourced by Macaw Media, except for: Dreamstime.com: Charles Knowles 12BL; Richardt777 27; Aleksandrs Kendenkovs 45.